Spooky Creature Riddles

Janet Nuzum Myers
Illustrated by Bob Ostrom

STERLING CHILDREN'S BOOKS
New York

For Warren, who chuckles at my jokes—even the groaners.

STERLING CHILDREN'S BOOKS
New York

An Imprint of Sterling Publishing
387 Park Avenue South
New York, NY 10016

STERLING CHILDREN'S BOOKS and the distinctive Sterling Children's Books logo are trademarks of Sterling Publishing Co., Inc.

ISBN 978-1-4027-8669-3 (paperback)

Library of Congress Cataloging-in-Publication Data

Myers, Janet Nuzum.
 Spooky creature riddles / Janet Nuzum Myers ; illustrated by Bob Ostrom.
  p. cm.
 ISBN 1-4027-1872-1
 1. Riddles, Juvenile. 2. Halloween--Juvenile humor. I. Ostrom, Bob. II. Title.
PN6371.5.M94 2005
818'.60208--dc22

Distributed in Canada by Sterling Publishing
c/o Canadian Manda Group, 165 Dufferin Street
Toronto, Ontario, Canada M6K 3H6
Distributed in the United Kingdom by GMC Distribution Services
Castle Place, 166 High Street, Lewes, East Sussex, England BN7 1XU
Distributed in Australia by Capricorn Link (Australia) Pty. Ltd.
P.O. Box 704, Windsor, NSW 2756, Australia

For information about custom editions, special sales, and premium and corporate purchases, please contact Sterling Special Sales at 800-805-5489 or special-sales@sterlingpublishing.com.

Manufactured in the United States of America
Lot #:
2   4   6   8   10   9   7   5   3   1
06/12
www.sterlingpublishing.com/kids

Contents

1 Ghosts

What do ghosts say when being introduced?
  "How do you boo?"

What's a good gift for a baby ghost?
  Booties.

What day of the week do ghosts prefer?
  Moan-day.

What do you call adult ghosts?
Groan-ups.

What do you call a ghost who lives in California?
A coast ghost.

What's a ghost's favorite snack?
Boo-berry muffins.

What do you call a ghost having a Halloween party?
A host ghost.

What do you call a ghost who pops all the party balloons?
A ghost buster.

What do you call a house-cleaning ghost?
A ghost duster.

What do you call a ghost who brags?
A ghost boaster.

What's a North Pole ghost's favorite dessert?
Ice scream.

How do you compliment a girl ghost?
"You look boo-tiful!"

How do you compliment a boy ghost?
"You look frightful!"

Where does a baby ghost sit?
In a booster seat.

Why did the ghost stay in bed all day?
Because he was as white as a sheet.

Why do ghosts fly?
To keep spirits high.

How do you bathe little ghosts?
Give them boo-ble baths.

Why wouldn't the ghost stay in the haunted house?
He was just passing through.

What did the ghost contestant get for last place?
The booby prize.

Why did the ghosts argue?
They were having a spirited debate.

Where do ghost military recruits go?
Boo camp.

What do teenage ghosts have?
A booooom box.

What happens when it rains on a haunted house?
Spirits are dampened.

Why are ghosts bad at typing?
Because they just haunt and peck.

How is a ghost like a soap bubble?
Both can quickly disappear.

Why did the ghost turn down an offer to dance?
He was dead on his feet.

Who did the beautiful ghost princess marry?
The haunt-some prince.

Where do country ghosts keep their boats?
In the boondocks.

What kind of books do ghosts read?
Boo-it-yourself books.

What do you call a ghost with a bell?
A dead ringer.

2 More Ghosts

Why are ghosts bad gamblers?
Because they don't have a ghost of a chance.

What signs do farmers post to keep ghosts away?
No haunting allowed.

What do you call a ghost safari?
A big game haunt.

Where do ghosts mail letters?
At the ghost office.

Who delivers mail for ghosts?
The ghost-man.

Why does mail for ghosts rattle?
Because they get chain letters.

What does a ghost use for hunting?
A boo and arrow.

Where do fashion-conscious ghosts
shop?
At boo-tiques.

What equipment do ghost firemen use?
Haunted hoses.

What lives with ghosts and eats cheese?
A haunted house mouse.

What is a ghost's slogan?
Now you see me, now you don't.

What do you get when a ghost stands too close to a
campfire?
A ghost roast.

What happened when a little ghost fell down?
He got a small boo-boo.

Why do ghosts go to baseball games?
To boo the umpires.

What's a ghost's favorite baseball team?
The Toronto Boo Jays.

How do you catch a ghost?
With a booby trap.

Why do ghosts like the Old West?
Because there are lots of ghost towns.

Where do nutty ghosts go?
To the booby hatch.

Why are ghosts good dancers?
They can boogie woogie.

What is a ghost's favorite kind of music?
Rhythm and Boos.

Why do actors avoid ghosts?
They don't want to get stage fright.

What did the couch potato ghost do all day?
Watched the boob tube.

What did the ghost bride carry?
A boo-quet.

What do ghosts wear in the snow?
Boots.

How do ghosts go upstairs in a haunted house?
The use the scare-case.

Where do ghosts sit in restaurants?
In booths.

What's a good gift for an Australian ghost?
A boomerang.

How do ghosts cross a busy street?
They wait until the ghost is clear.

Why did the ghost go to school?
To get a dead-ucation.

What did the ghost study in school?
Boo-ology.

Why was the ghost selected as a cheerleader?
Because of her school spirit.

What did the ghost use to move a huge pile of dirt?
A boo-dozer.

What's white and red all over?
An embarrassed ghost.

What do you call a ghost bee?
A boo-mble bee.

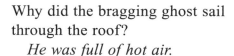

Why did the bragging ghost sail through the roof?
He was full of hot air.

Why was the ghost lonely in Korea?
He didn't know a Seoul.

What does a ghost say when asked how she's feeling?
"I'm all white."

Why was the ghost unhappy at the dance?
He had no body to dance with.

What does a ghost soldier on guard duty say?
"Halt! Who ghosts there?"

Why do ghosts like to ride in elevators?
It raises their spirits.

Where do stylish ghosts get their hair done?
At the boo-ty parlor.

What do little ghosts chew?
Boo-ble gum.

How do ghosts go on vacation?
They cruise on ghost ships.

What did the ghost say to everyone in the car?
"Boo-kle up."

3 Ghosts and Spooks

What's a ghost's favorite food?
Spook-ghetti.

How do ghosts decorate for a Halloween party?
With boo-lloons and screamers.

What branch of the service did the ghost join?
The Ghost Guard.

What do you call a crowd of ghosts watching a ballgame?
Spook-tators.

How does a ghost describe something that's wonderful?
"Spook-tacular!"

What do you call a ghost giving a speech at a banquet?
The guest spook-er.

What's a ghost's favorite city?
Spook-ane, Washington.

Why did the ghost sell fireworks?
He wanted a booming business.

What would you find in ghosts' libraries?
Dead silence.

What do you get if you cross a ghost and a dog?
A haunting dog.

Monsters and Mummies

Why was the monster tiptoeing and carrying a young chicken?

He thought he was supposed to walk softly and carry a big chick.

What do you call a monster in jail?
Mon-stir-crazy.

How can you tell that a monster enjoys scaring people?
He's grinning from fear to fear.

Why did the headless monster chase marathon runners?
He wanted to get ahead.

What did the monster give his headless girlfriend?
A neck-less.

Why did the monster detective stay in bed all day?
He wanted to stay under cover.

What do you call a monster who is just waking up?
Mon-stirring.

Why couldn't the monster catch a ball?
He was all thumbs.

What do monsters order at Chinese restaurants?
Mon-stir-fries.

What do you call a monster who never knocks at doors?
The Knock Less Monster.

What did the monster's house look like?
It was a monster-osity.

Why did the monster wear a large toupee?
He wanted to be a big wig.

What do you call Frankenstein hosting a talent show?
The monster of ceremonies.

Where did the mad scientist get Frankenstein's body parts?
Here, there, and everywhere.

How was Frankenstein created?
By trial and terror.

What did Frankenstein say when the mad scientist turned on the electricity?
"I'm shocked!"

Why couldn't Frankenstein get a credit card?
He was already charged to the limit.

Why was Frankenstein fascinated by electricity?
He liked current events.

Why did Frankenstein watch lightning?
He got a charge out of it.

Why did Frankenstein wreck his auto?
He wanted new body parts.

Why did Frankenstein act weird?
His brain was previously possessed.

Why was Frankenstein's brain returned to its owner?
It was repossessed.

Why did someone donate a brain to Frankenstein?
It was a no-brainer.

Why did the mummy miss the
Halloween party?
He was all wrapped up.

What's a mummy's favorite day of
the week?
Mum-day.

What's a mummy's favorite music?
Wrap.

Why are mummies popular at Halloween parties?
Because they are good wrappers.

Why did the young mummy cry at school?
He missed his mummy and dead-y.

What did the mummy say when told a secret?
"Mum's the word."

Why don't mummies use doorbells?
Because they like to wrap at the door.

What did the archaeologist say to the tomb robber?
"Show me the mummy!"

How do mummies travel within cities?
They take wrapp-ed transit.

What's the title of the mummy's new book?
Mummies for Dummies.

More Monsters and Mummies

Why did the big-footed monster walk through the mud?
He wanted to make a big impression.

What do monsters take with their coffee?
Scream and sugar.

What happened to the contortionist monster?
He was all bent out of shape.

Why did the monster buy a new outfit?
He wanted to have a clothes encounter.

What do you call two-headed cattle?
Mon-steer.

What kind of horses do monsters like?
Nightmares.

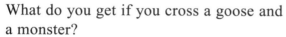

What game do little monsters like to play?
Hide and shriek.

What are monsters' favorite flowers?
Moaning gories.

What do you get if you cross a goose and a monster?
A mongoose, of course.

Why did the monster refuse to cross the unfinished bridge?
He heard it was held up by red tape.

Why did the monster chase the trolls from a room?
He wanted to make a troll-free phone call.

Why does a monster bellow when it's hurt?
When it pains, it roars.

When you see two vicious monsters, what do you call the smaller one?
The lesser of two evils.

What do you get if you cross a monster and a cobra?
I don't know, but if it hisses, run!

Why was Frankenstein an unhappy father?
His children were monsters.

What does Frankenstein read each day?
His horror-scope.

How was Frankenstein's brain like lightning?
One bright flash and it was gone.

How does Frankenstein like his eggs?
Terri-fried.

How can you tell when a mummy is worried?
He's tied up in knots.

What happens when a young mummy misbehaves?
He is sent to his tomb.

Why can't mummies run fast?
Their feet get tangled.

What do you call a mummy
who plays card games,
like gin?
*A rummy
mummy.*

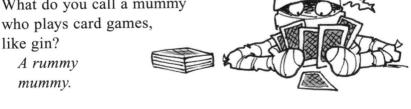

What do you call a mummy who steps in chewing gum?
A gummy mummy.

Why are mummies bad singers?
Because they are tomb deaf.

Why did the mummy stop singing?
He couldn't carry a tomb.

What does a mummy look like to a ghoul?
A yummy mummy.

What do you call a friendly mummy?
A chummy mummy.

What do you call a mummies' discussion group?
A wrap session.

What does a mummy wear on Halloween?
Masking tape.

How do mummies make sales pitches?
They offer to double your mummy back.

Frightening Figures

What do you call a monster's great artwork?
A monster-piece.

What's scary, ugly, and blue?
A monster holding its breath.

What watery creature never learns to tell time?
The Clock-Less Monster.

How are monsters picked for horror movies?
They are given a scream test.

When are mummies like birthday presents?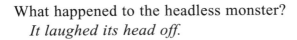
When they are gift-wrapped.

What's a good gift for a ten-foot monster?
Five pairs of shoes.

What happened to the headless monster?
It laughed its head off.

What did the monster eat after getting its tooth pulled?
The dentist.

What state did the monster come from?
It was a Vermont-ster.

What's a mummy's favorite breakfast?
Shrouded wheat.

Why did the mummy take a vacation?
So he could unwind.

Why are mummies good at keeping secrets?
Because they keep things under wraps.

What do monsters do in their spare time?
They watch wide-scream TV.

What do you get if you cross a mummy and Batman?
The Taped Crusader.

Other Spooky Creatures

What do bats do in their spare time?
They just hang around.

Why did the bat gargle mouthwash?
He had bat breath.

How did the bat get on the baseball team?
He was a good batter.

Why did the bat get kicked off the baseball team?
His batting average went down.

What's a black cat's favorite color?
Purr-ple.

What does a black cat drink on Halloween?
A bowl of scream.

How did the newlywed black cats monogram their towels?
Hiss and Purrs.

Where do you find a black cat in an orchestra?
In the purr-cussion section.

How do you compliment a black cat?
Tell her she's purr-ty.

What do you call an out-of-control black cat?
Hiss-terical.

What did the black cat score on his test?
Purr-fect.

What do you get if you cross a black cat and a coffeepot?
A purr-colator.

What happened to the black cat that fell into a barrel of pickles?
Curiosity dilled the cat.

Why do black cats make bad friends?
They are catty.

What do you call a single file of dancing black cats?
A feline dance.

What's a black cat's best subject?
Hiss-tory.

What do black cats say when they are parting?
"Have a mice day."

What do you call a jack-o'-lantern that is good at sports?
A jock-o'-lantern.

What do you call a talented, versatile jack-o'-lantern?
A jack-of-all-trades-o'-lantern.

What do you call a jack-o'-lantern that hops?
A jackrabbit-o'-lantern.

What do you call a jack-o'-lantern that wins the lottery?
A jackpot-o'-lantern.

How do you compliment a jack-o'-lantern?
Tell it it's glowing.

What do you get if you cross a pancake and a pumpkin?
A flapjack-o'-lantern.

What do you call a jack-o'-lantern that pops up and down?
A jack-in-the-box-o'-lantern.

Why did the spiders get engaged?
They wanted to web.

When are the spiders getting married?
They want a big June webbing.

Why do spiders eat corn?
So they can make cobwebs.

Why was the spider driving a little car?
She was just spinning her wheels.

Why are spiders good at baseball?
They know how to catch flies.

What game do little girl spiders play?
I spied-her.

Where do spiders learn English?
In Webster's.

What happened to the spider that claimed she made another spider's web?
She was caught in her web of lies.

Little Miss Muffet should have said what to the spider?
"Bug off!"

Why is it hard to believe what spiders say?
They spin the truth.

More Spooky Creatures

Where does a bat take a shower?
In the bat-room.

Where does a bat soak?
In a bat-tub.

What does a bat wear after it bathes?
A bat-robe.

What is written on a sign that points to a bat cave?
Hang in there.

What do bats eat?
Alpha-bat soup.

What do you call an old, mean female bat?
A battle axe.

How do you help a tired bat?
Recharge its batteries.

What do you call a fight between two bats?
Combat.

What do you call a fight among several bats?
A battle.

What noise do fighting bats make?
Battle cries.

What kind of boat do bats prefer?
A battleship.

What game do bats play?
Bat-minton.

What do you serve black cats at a Halloween party?
Cake and mice cream.

What did the black cat give her boyfriend at the end of their date?
A good-night hiss.

Why wouldn't the black cat tell his girlfriend any secrets?
She might hiss and tell.

Where do black cats shop?
In catalogs.

Why did the black cat order a computer?
She heard it came with a mouse.

What do you call it when a black cat buys something?
A purr-chase.

What do you call a humongous heap of black cats?
A meow-tain.

What do you call someone who steals black cats?
A cat burglar.

What do you call a black cat that lives in the mountains?
A meow-taineer.

What's a black cat's favorite song?
*She'll Be Coming Around the
Meow-tain.*

Where does a black cat carry her
money?
In her purr-se.

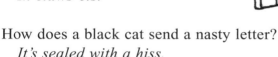

Where do black cats hide?
In claws-ets.

How does a black cat send a nasty letter?
It's sealed with a hiss.

What do you call a list of black cat baseball players?
The fe-lineup.

Why did the old black cat become a mother?
She got a litter in the mail.

What game did the black cat's kittens play?
Follow the litter.

What did the black cat give the kittens?
Hugs and hisses.

Why did the black cat refuse to ride in a car?
She had claws-trophobia.

What kind of music do black cats like?
Claws-i-cal.

What do you say to a jack-o'-lantern with luggage?
"Where are you glowing?"

What do you call a cold jack-o'-lantern?
Jack Frost-o'-lantern.

What do you see when you turn a jack-o'-lantern around?
A back-o'-lantern.

What do you call an unhappy jack-o'-lantern?
A sad-sack-o'-lantern.

What do you call a jack-o'-lantern that gambles?
A blackjack-o'-lantern.

What do you have when you lose a jack-o'-lantern?
A lack-o'-lantern.

How can you tell that a jack-o'-lantern likes candles?
Its face lights up.

How can you tell that a jack-o'-lantern hates the wind?
Its face darkens.

How do you repair a jack-o'-lantern?
With a pumpkin patch.

What do you call an overweight jack-o'-lantern?
A plump-kin.

What do you get if you cross a jack-o'-lantern and a rabbit?
A jackrabbit with a very bright face.

What do you call a jack-o'-lantern made of wood?
A lumberjack-o'-lantern.

Why did the spider get dizzy?
She was spinning too fast.

What's a spider's favorite game?
Spin the bottle.

Where do spiders keep their computers?
At web-sites.

Why did the spider take a laptop to the beach?
So she could surf the web.

9 Bats, Black Cats, and More

What kind of bat performs in a circus?
An acrobat.

What do you get if you cross a bat and a bell?
A dingbat.

When did the young bat's mother meet his teacher?
At bat-to-school night.

Why do black cats sing on Halloween?
Because they are mews-ical.

Why do black cats like Halloween?
Because of the mice-querade parties.

What game do black cats play at a Halloween party?
Mews-ical chairs.

Where did the black cat move?
He moved fur away.

What stories do black cats read to kittens?
Furry tales.

How do bats cook their food?
In flying pans.

What prize did the black cat win?
An A-cat-emy Award.

Why is it hard to understand black
cats from different countries?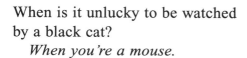
They speak fur-eign languages.

When is it unlucky to be watched
by a black cat?
When you're a mouse.

What do black cats eat for breakfast?
Mice Crispies.

What do you call a black cat's sparkly
jewelry?
Kitty glitter.

What kind of car does a black cat drive?
A Cat-illac.

What magazines do black cats read?
Mews-week and Good Mouse-keeping.

What do you get if you cross a jack-o'-lantern and a
chef?
Pumpkin pie.

What do dizzy, confused spiders say?
"Oh, what tangled webs we weave!"

What was the spider told after her job interview?
"Don't crawl us—we'll crawl you."

Skeletons, Goblins, and Ghouls

Why was the skeleton such a coward?
He didn't have any guts.

Why did the skeleton couple buy two cars?
They wanted a his and hearse.

Who did the nutty skeleton think he was?
Napoleon Bone-apart.

Why don't skeletons like dogs?
They bury their bones.

What's a good wedding gift for a skeleton?
Bone china.

What do you say to a skeleton who is going on a trip?
"Bone voyage."

Why do skeletons laugh a lot?
It's easy to tickle their funnybones.

What do you call a skeleton rock music group?
The Rolling Tombstones.

What do you get if you cross a skeleton and a groundhog?
An animal too thin to see its own shadow.

Why don't skeletons go to school?
Because they are boneheads.

Why did the skeleton stay up all night?
He had to bone up for an exam.

Why was the skeleton mad at the other skeleton?
He had a bone to pick with him.

What do you call a skeleton's pay raise?
A bone-us.

What do you call a goblin who makes shoes?
A cobblin' goblin.

How did the goblin get wet at a Halloween party?
He was an apple-bobbin' goblin.

After breaking both legs, why did the goblin lose arguments?
He didn't have a leg to stand on.

What do you call a goblin who cries?
A sobbin' goblin.

What do you call a goblin on crutches?
A hobblin' goblin.

What do you call a goblin who
overeats?
A gobblin' goblin.

What do you feed a sad goblin?
Cheery pie.

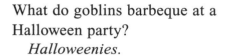

What do goblins barbeque at a
Halloween party?
Halloweenies.

Who provided cookies at the Halloween party?
The Ghoul Scouts.

How does a ghoul find a friend in the cemetery?
He sees what he can dig up.

What did the ghoul dig up?
A ghoul-friend.

What did the ghoul-friend say when the ghoul asked her
to marry him?
"Of corpse I will!"

Why did the ghoul have digestive problems?
He had ghoul-stones.

What do you call a girl ghoul pictured on the front of a
magazine?
A cover ghoul.

What do ghoul gardeners grow?
Tomb-atoes.

What's a ghoul's favorite drink?
Ghoul-ade.

What do you get if you cross a "hip" ghoul and a cat?
A real ghoul cat.

Why was the ghoul picked for the soccer team?
He was a good ghoulie.

Why do ghouls play soccer?
Just for kicks.

Why do ghouls' faces look sad?
Because of their grave expressions.

What do ghouls call a hearse?
Meals on wheels.

More Skeletons, Goblins, and Ghouls

Which skeleton won the race?
It was a dead heat.

Why did the skeleton lose the race?
His heart wasn't in it.

How do skeletons lock doors?
With deadbolts.

Why do skeletons make bad liars?
Because you can see right through them.

What do you call it when a skeleton miner strikes gold?
A bone-anza.

How does a skeleton get into a locked cemetery?
With a skeleton key.

How did the skeleton keep warm?
He built a bone-fire.

What instruments do skeletons play?
Trombones.

What do you call the night workers in a cemetery?
The graveyard shift.

Who works the graveyard shift in a cemetery?
Just a skeleton crew.

What do you call a skeleton that refuses to work?
Lazybones.

Why do skeletons sleep?
Because they are dead tired.

Where do skeletons swim?
In the Dead Sea.

What's a skeleton's favorite food?
Ribs.

What did the French waiter say to the skeleton when serving his meal?
"Bone appétit!"

What do you call a skeleton that owes money?
A deadbeat.

Why did the coward skeleton walk in reverse?
He was trying to show some backbone.

Why do skeletons stay out of the rain?
To avoid being soaked to the bone.

Why did the goblin's bicycle keep falling over?
Because it was two-tired.

What do you call a goblin who steals?
A robbin' goblin.

What do you call a stuck-up goblin?
A snob goblin.

What do you call a crowd of rioting goblins?
Mob-lins.

What did the party host goblin say as he offered a tray of cookies?
Treat or trick?

What's a ghoul's favorite side dish?
Human beans.

What do ghouls wear on rainy days?
Ghoul-ashes.

What did the ghoul win at the Olympics?
A ghoul medal.

What do you get if you cross a ghoul and King Midas?
A ghoul-d digger.

Why did the ghoul advertise free cemetery plots?
It was a dead giveaway.

How popular are cemeteries?
People are dying to get in.

What do you call roads in cemeteries?
Dead ends.

How is a ghoul like an apple?
Both are rotten to the core.

What's a ghoul's favorite flower?
Mari-ghouls.

What kind of jewels do ghouls wear?
Tombstones.

What's a little ghoul's favorite pet?
A ghoul-fish.

What's a little ghoul's favorite story?
Ghoul-ilocks and the Three Scares.

What's the favorite word of a ghoul who delays or puts things off?
Tomb-orrow.

What's a ghoul's slogan?
Leave no tombstone unturned.

What's a ghoul's favorite food?
Ghoul-ash.

What does a ghoul put on his goulash?
Grave-y.

Awesome Creatures

What do you call a skeleton in a refrigerator?
Chilled to the bones.

What do you get if you cross a skeleton and a genie?
Wishbones.

What expression do skeletons wear on their faces?
Deadpan.

What's a good gift for a little skeleton?
A dead-dy bear.

How did the skeleton predict rainstorms?
He felt it in his bones.

What do you call a skeleton in a swimming pool?
A skinny-dipper.

Why did the food quickly disappear at the Halloween party?
Everybody was a goblin.

What position did the goblin play in the baseball game?
He played in fright field.

What wears skates and lots of padding?
An ice hockey ghoul-ie.

What's a ghoul's favorite dance?
The vaults.

What game do young ghouls play?
Corpse and robbers.

13 Vampires

What keeps vampires healthy?
Bite-amins.

Why did the vampire run away after biting another vampire?
It was a bit-and-run accident.

Why was the vampire so tired?
His bat-tery was low.

What do you call Count Dracula after he falls down the stairs?
A black-and-blueblood.

Why did Dracula go to school?
So he could learn to count.

Why is Dracula considered to be intelligent?
Because he can think outside the box.

What did the vampire get when he attacked a snowman?
Frostbite.

What food is bad for a vampire's heart?
Steak.

Why are vampires good at baseball?
They can turn into bats.

Why was the vampires' baseball game canceled?
The bats flew away.

What did the vampire say after going to the dentist?
"I don't have a fang to wear!"

What do you call a group of singing vampires?
A vam-choir.

Where did the vampire want to apply for a job?
The blood bank.

What did the vampire expect at the blood bank?
Fast food.

What did the vampire do after reading a blood bank's help-wanted ad?
He laughed all the way to the bank.

What was the vampire told at the blood bank?
"We don't keep your type here."

Why did the vampire *give* blood at the blood bank?
He had transfusion confusion.

What do you say to Dracula when he wins a prize?
"Con-dracula-tions!"

Why do vampires hang around boat docks?
They are looking for blood vessels.

What's a vampire's favorite fruit?
Neck-tarines.

What's a vampire's favorite pet?
A bloodhound.

How do you avoid Dracula's cold?
Stay away from his coffin.

What helps Dracula when he has a cold?
Coffin drops or coffin syrup.

Why doesn't anyone like Count Dracula?
He's a pain in the neck.

What do you call it when Dracula is resting in his coffin?
A countdown.

Why was Dracula grumpy?
He woke up on the wrong side of the coffin.

How did grumpy Dracula get out of his coffin?
He flipped his lid.

What magazine do vampires read?
Vein-ity Fair.

Why are vampires computer nerds?
They have mega-bites.

Why did the vampire brothers fight?
There was bad blood between them.

Why did the vampire sweat when he saw his brother?
He made his blood boil.

What does a vampire do if he has only one fang?
He grins and bares it.

14 More Vampires

What happened when Count Dracula found a victim
shortly before sunrise?

He was just in the neck of time.

What do you have when Dracula takes too much blood
from his victim?

A-count overdrawn.

Why is the vampire getting married?
It was love at first bite.

What do you call a group of teenage vampires?
A fang gang.

Why do vampires make good fishermen?
They get lots of bites.

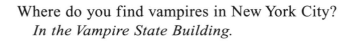

Where do you find vampires in New York City?
In the Vampire State Building.

Why do dentists put braces on vampires?
To fix their overbites.

What did the vampire think of the heiress?
She was too rich for his blood.

What advice did the vampire give his son?
"Don't bite the hand of the neck that feeds you."

Why did the vampire ditch his cruel girlfriend?
She had ice water in her veins.

Why was the vampire pinch hitter used only for night-time baseball games?
He could only strike at night.

Why did Count Dracula smoke?
He wasn't worried about another nail in his coffin.

How did Dracula get out of his nailed coffin?
  He was a nail biter.

Why is it impossible to destroy a vampire with a gun?
  He bites the bullet.

Why did the vampire carry a hammer, a knife, a baseball
a bat, and a big club?
  He wanted to be armed to the teeth.

How do you compliment a vampire?
  Tell him he's fang-tastic.

Why was Dracula fired from a job?
  He took too many coffin breaks.

Why did Count Dracula study all night?
His doctor said he was going to give him a blood test.

Why did the vampire become a vegetarian?
He thought he could squeeze blood out of a turnip.

Why does the vampire want relatives around?
He enjoys necks of kin.

When does a vampire invite relatives for dinner?
At Fangs-giving.

Why did Dracula hide in his coffin?
His life was at stake.

Why was Dracula claustrophobic?
He didn't like being boxed in.

Why don't vampires date girls from the Arctic?
They are too cold-blooded.

Why did the vampire want to join a secret organization?
He heard members became blood brothers.

Why did the vampire take an art class?
He wanted to draw blood.

What did the polite vampire say?
"Fangs very much."

Why is the cowardly vampire doomed?
He can't stand the sight of blood.

Why do vampires avoid stand-up comics?
They taste funny.

Why is it easy to trick vampires?
They are suckers.

What's a vampire's favorite fruit?
Vam-pears.

What happened to the vampire during a dust storm?
He bit the dust.

What type of blood does a vampire have?
Donated.

What did the vampire say to his girlfriend?
"I like your type."

What does Dracula drink when he gets up?
De-coffin-ated coffee.

What sport does Dracula play?
Casket-ball.

Why did the vampire try out for a play?
He wanted a bit part.

Why do vampires like daredevils?
Because they stick their necks out.

Why did the vampire and his girlfriend break up?
Because he loved her in vein.

A Few More Vampires

What drinks blood and has fangs and two wheels?
A vampire on a bicycle.

Why did the vampire follow Little Red Riding Hood?
He wanted to visit her neck of the woods.

Why did the vampire ride a racehorse?
Because he knew how to win by a neck.

What do you call a vampire who fell in a lake?
A damp-ire.

What was the name of the lake?
Lake Eerie.

What's Dracula's favorite movie?
Planet of the Capes.

Why did Count Dracula wear a black shawl?
His cape was at the cleaners.

What wears a cape, has fangs, and bounces?
Dracula on a trampoline.

Why did Dracula's wife want a divorce?
Because he stayed out all night.

What do you get if you cross Count Dracula and a duck?
Count Quack-ula.

16 Werewolves

What did the werewolf say when getting his first shave?
"Hair today, gone tomorrow."

What's a werewolf's favorite holiday?
Howl-loween.

Why do werewolves sleep all day?
Because they are night howls.

Why did the werewolf take his pet rabbit to the beauty shop?
He wanted to get his hare done.

Why do werewolves avoid NASCAR races?
Because they are such hair-raising events.

What do you call a werewolf in a Laundromat?
A wash-and-wear-wolf.

Why did the werewolf overfeed his pet rabbit?
Because his hare was getting thin.

Why did the werewolf separate his two rabbits?
He was splitting hares.

Why did the werewolf's rabbit run away?
To join the hare force.

What state has the most werewolves?
Moon-tana.

What is a werewolf's favorite time of the year?
The howl-idays.

What did the werewolf name his son?
Harry.

What do you call Harry's baby stroller?
Harry-carry.

What did the girl say to her werewolf boyfriend?
You fright up my life.

Why was the werewolf's hair noisy?
He had bangs.

What's a werewolf's favorite dog?
Irish Werewolfhound.

Why did the werewolf decide to sell shoes?
Because he heard there's no business like shoe business.

What did the hound dog say to the werewolf?
"Howl are you?"

Why did the private detective werewolf get a haircut?
*He wanted to be called
Shearlock Combs.*

Why did Shearlock Combs carry
luggage?
He liked open-and-shut cases.

What's a young werewolf's
favorite toy?
A were-wiffle ball.

What do you get if you cross a
werewolf and a tree?
A tree with a bite worse than its bark.

Why did the werewolf become the first werewolf to get a
haircut?
Because he was always on the cutting edge.

Why did the werewolf avoid the shady nightclub?
He heard it was a clip joint.

Why do werewolves carry keys?
They have lots of locks.

What do you call a werewolf wearing a wool sweater and
wool pants?
A werewolf in sheep's clothing.

How often do werewolves get together?
Just once in a blue moon.

Why was the werewolf bored?
He needed something new to sink his teeth into.

What instrument does a werewolf play?
Hair-monica.

Why was the werewolf foolish?
He had hair-brained ideas.

What do you call a werewolf in a coma?
An unaware-wolf.

What happened when the werewolf fell into a barrel of glue?
He was haired stiff.

17 More Werewolves

How are a werewolf and the wind alike?
  Both can howl.

Where do werewolves work?
  They just moonlight.

What's a werewolf's favorite airport?
  O'Hair Airport.

Why do werewolves think barbers are rude?
Because they make cutting remarks.

How did the werewolf like his new short haircut?
He thought it was shear magic.

What was the werewolf called after getting a short haircut?
Bob.

What happened when the werewolf drank starch?
He had a stiff upper lip.

What did the werewolf waiter say?
"I'm hair to please you."

What did the werewolf lifeguard say?
"I'm hair to save you."

What happened when the werewolf attacked a hippopotamus?
He bit off more than he could chew.

What do you call an Irish werewolf?
Mr. O'Haira.

Why was the werewolf proud of his son?
Because he was a howling success.

How does a werewolf answer a classroom roll call?
"I'm hair."

Why did the werewolf hide?
He was having a bad hair day.

Why are werewolves always late?
They avoid shortcuts.

Why was the werewolf unpopular?
Because of his hair-trigger temper.

Where does a werewolf spend the night?
At the Howl-iday Inn.

Why did the werewolf eat matches?
He was on a light diet.

What did the werewolf need on a windy day?
Scare spray.

How did the pet rabbit help the werewolf look good?
He loaned him his hare conditioner.

Why did the werewolf bid farewell to his pet rabbit?
His hare needed to be parted.

After his rabbit went away, what happened to the werewolf?
He was hareless.

What kind of dreams do werewolves have?
Bite-mares.

Why did the werewolf attack the tightrope walker?
He wanted a balanced diet.

Why was the werewolf itching?
He had shopped at a flea market.

Why do werewolves make bad magicians?
You can't teach an old werewolf new tricks.

What do you call a werewolf who is anxious and troubled?
A worry-wolf.

Why did the werewolf take his son to a babysitter?
To get him out of his hair.

Why can't you pet a werewolf?
You might rub him the wrong way.

What do you call a tired werewolf?
A weary-wolf.

Why did the werewolf attack skinny victims?
He was trying to eat smaller portions.

Why did the werewolf get a body perm?
He wanted to make waves.

What's a favorite game of werewolves?
Moon-opoly.

What did the werewolf say to the moon?
"You bring out the beast in me."

Why did the werewolf, armed with a bow and arrow, aim at the sky?

He was shooting for the moon.

Why did the werewolf attack the fastest runner in a race?

He wanted a quick bite.

What happens if you make a werewolf mad?

He might chew you out.

Why did the werewolf wear furry slippers?

Because his feet were bare.

Big, Bad Werewolves

How do werewolves mail letters?
Fierce class.

What did the werewolf say to his victim?
"It's nice to gnaw you."

What award did the werewolf win in the contest?
Fierce place.

How do werewolves send packages?
By hair-mail.

What do you get if you cross a werewolf and a duck?
A hairy critter that quacks at the moon.

What happened to the werewolf who wanted to be a movie star?
He went to Howl-lywood.

Why did the werewolf hang out in the clock shop?
To kill some time.

What do you call a werewolf who uses foul language?
A swear-wolf.

What do you call an angry werewolf?
A beware-wolf.

19 Witches

What do you call a young witch on a broom?
A baby broomer.

Why do witches on brooms wear seat belts?
So they don't fly off the handle.

How do witches on brooms keep the world clean?
They sweep the sky.

What do you hear when a witch breaks the sound barrier?
A sonic broom.

Why was the witch afraid to ride her broom?
She had feelings of broom and doom.

How do you compliment a witch?
Tell her she looks bewitching.

How does a witch tell time?
She looks at her witch-watch.

Why did the witch sell brooms?
It was a fly-by-night business.

How is a witch like a hen?
Both can cackle.

What's a witch's favorite city?
Witch-ita, Kansas.

What do you get if you cross a witch and a snowman?
A cold spell.

What do you get if you cross a witch and a fireman?
A hot spell.

How do witches send packages?
By FedHex.

What did the sports headline say about the witch who came off the bench to pitch the baseball game?
A Witch in Time Saves Nine.

What do you call an unhittable baseball thrown by a witch?
The wicked pitch of the witch.

Why are witches banned from gambling casinos?
Because of their blackjack magic.

What do you call a married witch?
A hitched witch.

What do you call a witch's broom with a loud muffler?
A ba-rooooom stick.

What do you call witches wearing slacks?
Witches in britches.

Why are witches good at croquet?
Because they are wicket witches.

What do you call a witch walking on a scenic trail?
A witch-hiker.

What do you call witches who can't stop laughing?
Witches in stitches.

What do you call witches' brew in Texas?
Tex-Hex.

84

What do you call a wart on the end of a witch's nose?
Her beauty mark.

What did the California witch call her candle shop?
The Wicked Wicks of the West.

What did the New York witch call her candle shop?
The Candle Shop. (Gotcha!)

Why did the frog hop quickly away from the witch?
He didn't want to be turned into a handsome prince.

Why did the witch buy hundreds of beehives?
She was bee-witched.

What do you call witches' handmade items?
Witchcrafts.

What book does a witch read to her kitten?
The Black Cat in the Pointed Hat.

Why did the witch hold tryouts for a spelling bee?
She likes to cast spells.

Why did the witch fasten a clock to her broom?
She wanted to see if time flies.

What did the witch learn from her clock experiment?
Time flies when she's having fun.

Why didn't the witch's train make stops?
It was the hex-press train.

Why do witches make bad photographers?
They have too much hocus-focus.

20 More Witches

How do witches learn to fly?
  They just wing it.

Why did the witch give up trying to ride her broom?
  She couldn't handle the ups and downs.

What advice was the witch given?
  "Straighten up and fly right!"

What do you call a witch on the beach?
A sand-witch.

What do you call a show-off witch on the beach?
A ham sand-witch.

What do you call a coward witch on the beach?
A chicken sand-witch.

What do you call a sunburned witch on the beach?
A toasted sand-witch.

What do you call a witch on the beach who is being asked a lot of questions?
A grilled sand-witch.

What do you call a mosquito bite on a witch?
A witch itch.

What do you call a witch on a safari?
A witch hunt.

What's another name for a witch?
A flying sorcerer.

What do you call bat bones, toads, lizard gizzards, and poisonous mushrooms?
Ingredients for a witch's brew.

How good was the witch's brew?
It was hex-tra special.

What is a romantic dinner for a witch?
Brew for two.

What did the witch think of her boyfriend?
She was spellbound.

Why was the witch tongue-tied around her boyfriend?
She couldn't hex-press herself.

Why did the witch fly to Holland?
Her boyfriend suggested they go Dutch.

What do you call a witch whose boyfriend breaks up with her?
A ditched witch.

What did the witch get when she slid off her broom?
Splinters.

What do you call it when a witch thinks she's beautiful?
Witch-ful thinking.

What's a witch's favorite song?
That Old Black Magic.

What's a witch's second-favorite song?
Bewitched, Bothered, and Bewildered.

How are identical twin witches confusing?
You can't tell witch is witch.

Why do witches ride brooms?
They just get swept away.

What magazine do witches read?
Vanity Fear.

What do you call it when a witch drives her Rolls Royce off the road and into a trench?
A rich witch in a ditch.

What does the young witch want to be when she grows up?
A witch doctor.

Why did the witch like St. Patrick's Day?
Because no one made fun of her green complexion.

What do you call it when witches can't sit still?
Witches' twitches.

Why did the witch buy a boat?
She wanted a new witch-craft.

What happened to the witch who fell into an upholstery machine?
She's now recovered.

Why did the witch stay in a hotel?
She liked the broom service.

What do you call it when a witch turns off all the lights?
Blackout magic.

What do you call it when a witch turns herself into something else?
A witch switch.

Why did the witch turn herself into a clown?
She was just clowning around.

Why did the witch enjoy turning into a clown?
It was her clowning achievement.

What do you call two witches sharing a house?
Broom-mates.

How does a witch drink tea?
From a cup and sorcerer.

Why did the witch's broom stay up all night?
It couldn't sweep.

21 Last Witches

What has four legs and flies?
   Two witches on a broom.

What do you call a witch who lost her broom and needs a ride?
   A witch-hiker.

What's a witch's favorite letter of the alphabet?
   The evil "I."

Why did the witch ride her broom through a car wash?
She wanted a clean sweep.

What did the witch say when asked if she changed the handsome prince into a frog?
"Of curse I did."

What jewelry does a witch wear?
A charm bracelet.

What do witches use to write letters?
Black Magic Markers.

Why was the witch late for school?
She had a good hex-cuse.

What do you get if you cross a witch and a winner of a spelling bee?
A magic speller.

How does a witch keep cool in hot weather?
She turns on the scare conditioner.

Why did the witch dig a deep hole in the ground?
She wanted to make a witching well.

When does a witch grant your special request?
When you witch upon a star.

What do you call a divorced witch?
The hex-wife.

How can you tell when a witch has a cold?
She has coughing spells.

Why did the witch put her broom to bed?
It was sweepy.

Where do witches relax?
On the golf curse.

When the witch refused to give up, what did she do?
She made a last-witch effort.

Index